Sir, the Days!

West Point July 1960–June 1964

William Robertson

outskirts
press

Sir, The Days!
West Point July 1960 - June 1964
All Rights Reserved.
Copyright © 2022 William Robertson
v3.0

The opinions expressed in this manuscript are solely the opinions of the author and do not represent the opinions or thoughts of the publisher. The author has represented and warranted full ownership and/or legal right to publish all the materials in this book.

This book may not be reproduced, transmitted, or stored in whole or in part by any means, including graphic, electronic, or mechanical without the express written consent of the publisher except in the case of brief quotations embodied in critical articles and reviews.

Outskirts Press, Inc.
http://www.outskirtspress.com

ISBN: 978-1-9772-5799-4

Cover Image by William Robertson

Outskirts Press and the "OP" logo are trademarks belonging to Outskirts Press, Inc.

PRINTED IN THE UNITED STATES OF AMERICA

Table of Contents

Prologue i

1	My Appointment to West Point	1
2	Plebe Summer – Beast Barracks	3
3	Plebe Year, First Semester	11
4	Plebe Year, Second Semester	26
5	Yearling Year Summer Training	32
6	Yearling Year First Semester (Fall 1961)	35
7	Yearling Year, Second Semester	38
8	Cow Year Summer Training – Beast Barracks Revisited	44
9	Cow Year, First Semester	48
10	Cow Year, Second Semester	53
11	First Class Year, Summer 1963	59
12	First Class Summer Training – Manheim, Germany	61
13	First Class Year, First Semester	68
14	First Class Year, Second Semester	77

Prologue

My motivation in writing this is to share this incredible experience with my wife Joan, our three daughters and grandchildren.

Ninety-five percent of us were not in the top 5% of our class in academics, and most of us were not first-string intercollegiate athletes. Only one in twenty-five would achieve one or more general stars, with an equal number coming from the top, middle and bottom of our class. Twenty-four classmates were killed in action in Vietnam.

Regardless of our academic standing or athletic achievement, what bonds us so deeply as a West Point class is that we all endured the same barrage of challenges and gained each other's mutual respect in the process.

While some of my experiences were unique to me, similar stories were commonplace. Most of the stories I wrote about were experiences we all shared. This is dedicated to my West Point class, the Class of 1964. Loyal friends and good men all.

Four Lifetime Takeaways

- Patriotism - The West Point Motto: "Duty, Honor, Country"
- Honor - The West Point Honor Code: "A cadet will not lie, cheat, steal or tolerate those who do."
- Leadership – The Code of Conduct: "If senior, I will take command."
- Accountability - A Plebe's Three Answers: "Yes sir, no sir and no excuse sir."

1

My Appointment to West Point

As I was growing up, I was drawn to the military, especially the Army. My heroes were all WWII soldiers. I played soldiers way more often than most boys. My dad and I watched every episode of "Victory at Sea" together. When I was in eighth grade, I saw the movie "To Hell and Back" with Audie Murphy playing himself, the most decorated soldier in American history. During my high school years I watched every episode of the "West Point" weekly TV series.

At Chaminade High School there was a very little office where college brochures were displayed. The office was manned by one of the teaching brothers during lunch hour and after class hours. I deliberately visited the office between classes as I did not want to be influenced one way or the other by the attending brother. I grabbed brochures from Boston College, Notre Dame, Georgetown, Manhattan College, St. Josephs, St. Bonaventure, and a pamphlet on how to apply for an appointment to a service academy. None of the brochures interested me. I knew what I wanted to do.

In order to attend a U.S. service academy, you had to apply for an appointment from your congressman or senator. The procedure involved filling out a form, with your SAT scores attached and a letter describing why you wanted to go to West Point or Annapolis. Not too long after I sent in my application, I received a letter from my congressman's office directing me to go to Mitchell Field Air Force Base for a medical and psychological exam, and while there I was also to take a civil service exam, which was an additional requirement of my congressman.

About a month later I received a letter advising me that I had received an alternate appointment. This meant that I would only get to attend West Point if the primary appointee decided not to go, or if one of the congressman's previous appointees washed out. I didn't know it at the time, but our congressman's principal appointment was given to future classmate John Ward who was a deserving honor student from St. Mary's High School in Manhasset. (John would be in the top 5% of our class in academics.) I hadn't given a lot of thought as to what my plan B would be. One plan was to attend Manhattan College. Another plan was to attend Nassau Community College for a year and re-apply for another appointment to West Point.

Unbeknownst to me, my congressman discovered that the congressman from Brooklyn had an unfilled appointment. I was contacted by the other congressman and asked to meet him for lunch at a restaurant in Manhasset. It was during school hours and I had on my sports jacket, which was obligatory dress at Chaminade. He asked me if I were interested in an appointment to Annapolis. I told him no and I thought that was the end of it.

Our senior prom was late in the year. As I was getting dressed for the occasion, my sister brought in the mail which included a letter from the congressman from Brooklyn congratulating me on my appointment to West Point. Perhaps him asking me if I would accept an appointment to Annapolis was only a test. I'll never know.

2

Plebe Summer – Beast Barracks

Beast Barracks, July - August 1960

After the Fourth of July weekend, my parents drove me to West Point where I would enter the Corps as a member of the class of 1964.

At the main gate, an MP signaled us to continue proceeding north on Thayer Road, where a drop-off area had been designated for such purpose. It was adjacent to the east portal (sallyport) which led into Central Area. I kissed my mom, shook hands with my dad, and walked forward through the portal to join the screaming chaos on the other side. Welcome to Beast Barracks.

The first 8 weeks of the West Point experience is called "Beast Barracks," which is an extremely intense part of your West Point experience. The squad leaders were "Cows" (rising juniors) and the cadet officers were all "Firsties" (rising seniors). They were totally responsible for all our training, and for them it was part of their leadership development training. They were very impressive, and their proficiency was intimidating. We were gross "smack heads," struggling with each new challenge.

The first day we were taught how to stand at attention, how to salute, how to "Report to the cadet with the red sash on," given all our medical shots, measured for our uniforms, given a buzz haircut, issued all of our gear, and taught the basics of marching in formation. "R-Day," as it came to be known, was programmed to be a very busy, efficient, and stressful day, and it checked all of those boxes.

The uniform for our last formation of the day was our summer dress uniform, which had been tailored while we were otherwise engaged. We didn't know all the positions in ranks, nor all of the marching commands, but we had been taught enough to be marched from central area, across the Plain to Trophy Point, where we would take the "Oath of Allegiance," and from there, marched directly to Washington Hall for our first supper as "new cadets."

> I, [name], do solemnly swear (or affirm) that I will support and defend the Constitution of the United States against all enemies, foreign and domestic; that I will bear true faith and allegiance to the same; that I take this obligation freely, without any mental reservation or purpose of evasion; and that I will well and faithfully discharge the duties of the office on which I am about to enter. So help me God.

Most of the training was given by the squad leaders. We were taught the manual of arms with a rifle, how to march with and without a rifle, how to disassemble, clean and reassemble your rifle, the "daily dozen" PT exercises, running in formation, bayonet drill, how to pack your field gear, how to pitch a tent, first aid, compass and map reading, how to put on and seal your gas mask in a chamber filled with CS gas, qualifying on the rifle range, and long marches up and down the hills with full field packs.

Most training sessions were one hour long and required changing uniforms between formations. The uniforms varied between gym clothes, short-sleeved Kaki's, cadet white shirts over grey trousers, or olive drab fatigues. There was barely enough time to change uniforms, put away the previous uniform where it belonged, and be back in ranks 5 minutes before the next formation. The pace was a deliberate stressor, and for me the rapid uniform change was one of the most challenging aspects of Beast Barracks.

Once in ranks, we would be standing at rigid attention, "bracing" with our chins tucked in. For the next 5 minutes we would be subject to inspection by the upperclassmen to see that we had gotten every component of the new uniform correct, and they challenged us with questions. One day, an upperclassman out of sight to my left asked a classmate, also out of my sight, "How many generals are there in the Army?" To which my unidentified classmate responded, "Sir, I do not know!" The upperclassman pressed on. "Plus or minus fifty smack head?" to which my classmate responded, "Plus fifty sir!" The upperclassmen reacted with, "You idiot!!" At this point the entire platoon was laughing and giggling while trying to maintain the proper position of attention. We were told to "Knock it off!" and the giggling stopped.

For the first month of Beast Barracks (July), our mid-morning event was "dismounted drill," where we marched around the Plain, first as individual squads and later in platoon formations. Picture 100 squads independently maneuvering, with 100 squad leaders barking commands, successfully avoiding colliding with one another. Commands reverberated across the expanse of the Plain. "Squad, right shoulder arms! Forward, march! Column left, march! Left shoulder, arms! Squad halt! Order, arms!" For the entire hour, a snare drummer and bass drummer from the West Point Army Band played continuously whatever crossed their minds, but never skipping a beat. While we were marching around in the sun, the drummers took advantage of a shade tree on the edge of the Plain. We were taught to listen to the drummers and were issued commands so that we would step off with the left foot on the beat of the bass drum. Having been a drummer in high school, I was fascinated with how really good these drummers were. At one point they launched into the "Army 2-4" which we had played in our spring band concert. I was so engrossed in listening to the drummers that I failed to hear the platoon leader's command and I continued to march straight ahead while the rest of the platoon executed column right. I suffered the appropriate level of verbal abuse.

On each day's training schedule, the hour before supper formation was for "group athletics," which was usually soccer or flag football. This sounded like fun and a respite from the other rigors of the day. Aside from the fun part, it also entailed running from the barracks to Target Field which is down by the river at the extreme north end of the post and running back up the hill to the barracks at the level of the Plain.

For meals there were ten people at each table. Two upperclassmen and eight new cadets. In those days while we ate, we had to "brace" (pull our chins back to our necks), sit on the front of our chairs, take little bites, thoroughly chewing and swallowing each bite before grasping our forks for the next bite. While we were eating, we were frequently interrupted by the upperclassmen testing our "Plebe knowledge," which we were supposed to learn in our non-existent free time. Failure to know the expected response resulted in "Sit up!" which meant this was likely to be the end of your meal. We all lost a lot of weight during Beast Barracks.

We were taught everything an enlisted soldier is taught in Basic Training, which included memorizing the Code of Conduct, which had been established in 1955 by executive order of President

Eisenhower. During the Korean War, some captured U.S. servicemen, lost their will to live and resist, and died in captivity as a result. The Code of Conduct was intended to address that.

> I am an American fighting man. I serve in the forces which guard my country and our way of life. I am prepared to give my life in their defense. I will never surrender of my own free will. If in command I will never surrender my men while they still have the means to resist. If I am captured I will continue to resist by all means available. ... I will keep faith with my fellow prisoners ... If I am senior, I will take command. If not, I will obey the lawful orders of those appointed over me ... When questioned, I am bound to give only name, rank, service number, and date of birth .... I will never forget that I am an American fighting man, responsible for my actions, and dedicated to the principles which made my country free. I will trust in my God and in the United States of America.

Besides learning what every soldier is taught in Basic Training, we had to memorize trivial facts about West Point, such as how many gallons in Luske Reservoir and how many lights in Cullum Hall. We had to learn West Point music: "The Corps", "The Alma Mater", "Army Blue", "Benny Havens", and "On Brave Old Army Team." When ordered to sing one of these songs, some renditions were so painfully bad, thereafter the upperclassmen just had that person recite the words. Other spirit songs to be learned were: "Fight Away," "Sons of Slum and Gravy," and "Black, Gold , Grey."

After supper there was an hour-long class, usually given by the senior cadet officers. This was when they covered the history and lore of West Point and all aspects of the Honor Code. "A cadet will not lie, cheat or steal, or tolerate someone who does."

The worst part of Beast Barracks was the shower formations which occurred at the end of the day, immediately after the last hour of instruction. The uniform was tee shirt, boxer shorts, bathrobes, and shower shoes (flip flops); a bar of soap in our right hand with a towel draped over our extended right arm. It was an hour of pure harassment, being screamed at, made to do pushups and having to run up and down the stairs repeatedly for not knowing some item of "Plebe knowledge" which we were expected to learn in our non-existent free time. Mercifully, the shower formation ended with each of us granted 15 seconds in the shower. Thank God they no longer do shower formations. The only constructive things I can think of was that the squad leaders inspected each of their squad member's feet and asked each new cadet if they had a bowel movement that day. This was a matter of concern as we had virtually no free time on the day's training schedule.

For the month of July, my first beast squad leader and platoon leader were very impressive, strict, and straight arrow as was expected, and as was 99.9% of the cadre. Not so my second beast squad leader, who in August erroneously thought I had given him the finger when he was introducing himself to his inherited squad. He was a sick SOB and he tried to run me out of the Corps. Among other things, he denied me 11 meals in a row. Given the amount of energy we were expending every day I thought I was going to die, but I was not going to let him run me out. I think his roommate, Jim Heldman, caught on to what Roger _____ was doing and intervened to put an end to it. Years later I would learn that then Captain Roger _____ had been discharged from the Army for conduct unbecoming an officer. That didn't surprise me. He never should have graduated from West Point.

The second to last week of Beast Barracks was spent qualifying on the rifle range. The last week was spent in the field, doing squad level maneuvers, and sleeping in two-man pup tents near Lake Frederick.

The last night at the Lake Frederick campsite, we gathered apart from the upper-class cadre and by a show of hands elected a class president and determined what would be our class motto. Our class president would be Dick Chilcoat, who came to West Point through the Army "Prep" school, which prepares selected, outstanding young soldiers for the academic rigors of West Point. Dick was a good choice and years later would become a 3-star General. The motto we chose was "Stars in Store for '64." General Westmoreland, who was Superintendent at that time, thought our motto was too precocious and suggested another. His suggestion was rejected and our motto remained "Stars in Store for '64."

The next morning, we marched with full field pack, 15 miles back to West Point. We were THE Class of 1964 and we had a motto to prove it.

The last week of August, the upperclassmen, who were not part of the Beast Barracks cadre, returned to West Point from their summer training or 30-day leave, the sequence of which depended upon their scheduling. The last event of Beast Barracks was the Acceptance Parade, which marked our transition from being "New Cadets" to being accepted as members of the Corps.

After the parade we were assigned to our cadet companies. I was assigned to H-2, (Company H, 2nd Regiment). Our class would be joined by 20 former members of the Class of 1963 who had been "turned back." These were cadets who had fallen a little short academically but were considered prime material to graduate from West Point and given another chance. (It should be noted that General George Patton was a "turn back.")

With the addition of 20 "turn backs," our class started with 799 people. In the course of our 4-year experience, 234 of the class would fail to meet the grade, either academically, physically, Honor Code violation, or due to lack of military aptitude as it was called. That is a failure rate of 30%.

3

Plebe Year, First Semester

The Barrack Areas and Regiments

There were three barracks areas: South Area, Central Area and North Area. (These have since been renamed after famous generals.) Each area was surrounded by a rectangle of barracks with a large, paved surface in the middle where the companies stood formation for reveille and meals and formed for parades.

There were two regiments, each consisting of 1,200 cadets. 1st Regiment was billeted in South Area and the south side of Central Area. The 2nd Regiment was billeted in North Area and the north side of Central Area. Company H-2 was located on the northwest corner of North Area.

Each regiment had 12 cadet companies consisting of about 100 cadets. Normally three Plebes shared a room. By Cow year (the third year), the ranks had thinned to the point where there were only two classmates assigned to a room.

The barracks in North and Central Areas were older and architected so that each "division" of barracks had four floors with four rooms on each floor. Each room had a sink and each floor had a shared bathroom (toilets/showers) at the end of the hall.

Company H-2

My first semester roommates were Bob Reich from Steelton, Pennsylvania, and Bob Wynn from Sevierville, Tennessee. Wynn's parents were divorced and he lived with his father who was a pharmacist. Reich was a football player. I believe his dad worked in the steel mill. I remember him telling the men would bet their paychecks on the Friday night high school games.

A service road ran behind the barracks on the west side of North Area. Our room was on the second floor and the service road emerged from a tunnel that passed under our room. Our window faced the gymnasium which was on the other side of the road.

The Honor Code

In Beast Barracks we had been subjected to several sessions related to the cadet Honor Code. "A cadet does not lie, cheat or steal, or tolerate someone who does."

The Honor Code and system were rigorously enforced by the cadet corps and cherished by both the current Corps of Cadets and the Long Grey Line of graduated alumni. We were taken at our word in all things, and the system depended upon that. If someone was prone to lie or cheat, there were frequent opportunities to do that because you were assumed to be a man of your word.

Each cadet company had an honor rep for each class year, with the honor rep having been voted to that position by their classmates in the company. If we observed someone lying or cheating we were honor bound to turn them in to our honor rep. The issue was turned over to a meeting of the cadet honor board, and If the person was found guilty, they were immediately escorted to the West Point Hospital where they would stay until their termination paperwork was completed. We lost two H-2 classmates to honor violations.

Plebe Duties

Six days a week the reveille cannon was fired at 5:50 AM. In each Area (North, South and Central) an Army Band bugler and drummer were positioned in a sallyport facing that area. When the canon went off, they began playing the 10-minute reveille formation drum-and-bugle call. Plebes were already up doing their assigned chores, but the upperclassmen stayed in bed until the five-minute mark.

One of the Plebe duties was being "Minute Caller." Each area of barracks had a guardhouse, with a Cow on guard duty who was responsible for displaying a flag indicating the uniform for the next formation. Each floor in the barracks had a "minute caller" whose job was to check the uniform flag and announce that to the people on his floor for each of five minutes until formation time.

Dozens of minute callers could be heard, the sound reverberating across the barracks area. For example: "Sir, there are five minutes until breakfast formation. The uniform is as for class with raincoats. Five minutes sir."

Each cadet room was required to subscribe to both the "New York Times" and the "Herald Tribune."

The newspapers were delivered to the barracks area and one of the

Plebe duties was to retrieve the newspapers for the people on their floor and to deliver them to each room between reveille and breakfast formation. We were not allowed to have a radio in our room the first semester of Plebe year so the newspapers were our only source of information. At breakfast we were questioned about the national and international headlines. As future soldiers, we were expected to keep abreast of what was going on in the world. Local politics was of no interest.

Since there was only one Plebe room on each floor, on any given week one of you would be the minute caller and another would be picking up and distributing the newspapers to the rooms on your floor.

There were several other Plebe duties and there just was not enough time between classes, intramurals and supper formations to get them all done. Some upperclassmen wanted to hear a synopsis of that night's movie and who starred in it, while other upperclassmen wanted to know who the officer of the day was tomorrow, and another wanted a report on the football team we were playing next Saturday. You and your Plebe company mates quickly learned that to survive, you had to cooperate and delegate amongst yourselves. Clandestine meetings were held which resulted in one classmate being dispatched to the post movie theater, another to the post guardhouse and another dispatched to the library. The results of their findings were disseminated to the Plebe rooms on each floor. This was an undocumented lesson in delegation and time management which every class had to learn for themselves.

Academics

Our first class began at 7:45 AM. Our last class of the day ended at 3:15 PM. We had two academic classes and gym in the morning and two academic classes in the afternoon. We even had two classes Saturday morning before the parade.

Most of our classes were in Thayer Hall which was very modern inside. The exterior was aged granite as it had been converted from the old horseback riding facility.

The number of students in each class was limited to 14. The cadet with the best grade sat in the first seat, and at the beginning rendered the report to the teaching officer "All present" or naming any cadets that were authorized to be absent. We then took seats to begin the class.

In first semester math we had algebra, geometry, trigonometry, and analytic geometry. It helped that I had taken these courses in high school, with analytic geometry being an advanced math course, but here we covered four years of high school math in one semester. Second semester math was calculus I.

In English we had reading, composition and speech making. The grading of our compositions was severe with a tenth off for every infraction of spelling, grammar, paragraph separation or imprecise selection of adjectives. I was often shocked to receive a C+ on a paper I thought worthy of a much better grade.

We all had to take a foreign language and the choices were German, French, Russian, Portuguese and Spanish. I took Spanish, which was considered to be the easiest and which I had taken in high school. With the challenges of Plebe year, I needed all the help I could get.

The Department of Earth Space and Graphic Sciences was located above Washington Hall which was our dining hall. Here we took mechanical drawing, surveying, earth science, world geography and astronomy. Early in the fall we went outside to survey the Plain. There were several legs to the course and your grade depended upon how close you came to the actual elevation at the last post.

Military tactics class was given in Thayer Hall, and as one would expect, physical education classes were held in the gym, where we had boxing, wresting, gymnastics and survival swimming.

We were graded every day on every subject and at the end of the week our grades were publicly posted in the sallyport, designated for our class year. (The sallyports were the portals into the barracks areas.) Before supper on Friday, we had to copy our grades and record them on a form kept on the door of our clothing locker. This was so when our company TAC officer inspected our room, he could see how we were doing in academics.

We were expected to maintain a passing grade in every subject and if you failed to remain "proficient" in all subjects, you lost your weekend privileges, which meant you were not allowed to "drag" (have a date) Saturday or Sunday and you were confined to your room after supper Saturday night and after lunch on Sunday, to encourage you to study more. You were getting a free education and there was no free ride.

Besides being graded every day, there were partial reviews (tests) and finals at the end of the semester.

At the end of the semester, If your accumulative grade in any subject was deficient, you were given a retry "turnout" exam in that subject. If you failed that, you were "turned out" and sent packing.

Plebe Boxing

Teaching right-handed people how to attack and defend against left-handers was too advanced for our one-semester boxing course, so we were all taught to fight right-handed. This put us lefties at a disadvantage. It was not natural and my right cross was weak. The assignment of opponents was arbitrarily made at the moment by our instructors, Mr. Creighton and Joe "Punchy" Palone. One of my bouts was against Gary Lavoy. I was 5'9" and Gary was well over 6' tall. We were scored on a modified Olympic system: one point for a jab, 2 points for landing a right cross and 3 points for a knockdown, as I recall. The bell sounded and Gary started pumping my face with a steady barrage of left jabs, steadily racking up the points, while I couldn't reach him. Instinctively I tried to turn around to fight left handed, but each time I was sternly instructed to resume the right-hand position. This pounding went on for 3 rounds, only limited by Gary's endurance. I don't think I ever laid a glove on him. The next class was math in Thayer Hall. After we were told to "take boards," the instructor noticed I was just standing there in a trance, not working the problem. He approached me, turned me around, looked at my face and eyes and told me to sit down. I was not graded that day.

Plebe Year Intramurals

Soldiering is a physical endeavor, and every cadet was expected to be an athlete. The cadet companies fielded intramural teams that competed in fall, winter, and summer sports. If you were on an intercollegiate team you were absolved from the intramural program for that season.

In the fall there was tennis, 8-man tackle football, soccer and track. The intramural winter sports were wrestling, basketball, water polo and handball. I recall baseball, lacrosse, tennis, and golf in the spring.

We had intramurals 4 days a week: Monday, Tuesday, Thursday and

Friday. There was a practice parade before supper on Wednesday. Our last academic class ended at 3:15 PM, at which point we returned to our barracks to change into our sports uniform. The teams gathered in front of the barracks at 4 PM and then we walked to the gym or ran to the field designated for that sport.

The first classmen of the company decided what intramural sports team you were on, and each team was led by one of the Firsties. Plebe year, In the fall I was on the company track team. The winter sports were wrestling, basketball, water polo and handball. I was assigned to the water polo team which was horrible – 60 minutes of drowning.

On the company track team I ran the 880 and 880 relay. The only meet I can recall is the one where I had to run against Larry Bedell, who had run track in high school and was recognized as one of the best runners in intramurals. Larry won the 880 but I came in second. In the 880 relay I was positioned to run against him again. Before the race my team captain threatened that I had better beat him this time. I stayed with him for most of the race, but when it came to passing the baton, he was one stride ahead of me. I stretched forward to pass the baton successfully, but my momentum carried me forward and I skidded face down on the cinders scratching my arms, hands and nose. My team captain happened to be the senior person on my dining table and at supper he had me "sit up" because I had lost my leg of the race.

SAMI (Saturday Morning Inspection)

Besides studying for our Saturday morning classes, on Friday nights we had to prepare our room for Saturday Morning Inspection, which was commonly referred to as "SAMI."

Each cadet company had a TAC officer (usually a major or soon-to-be-promoted captain) who was responsible for overseeing the cadet chain of command and mentoring and guiding all of us. One of his duties was to inspect our rooms while we were in Saturday morning classes.

The room had to be spotlessly clean and every item in its prescribed location. One roommate was designated as the "room corporal" for the week and he received all demerits related to the shared space. The TAC officer would inspect each of our clothing lockers to see that everything was in its prescribed place and to check our grades to see if we were "proficient" in all subjects. (Recall our grades had to be transcribed the evening before, from sheets publicly posted in our class sallyport.) Our TAC also inspected our field gear and parade uniforms which we had displayed in a prescribed manner on our beds.

Bob Reich's Concussion

Bob Reich played on the Plebe football. One Friday, after Wynn and I returned from intramurals, we discovered Reich sprawled on his bunk. Moaningly, he explained that he had been sent home from practice, having sustained a concussion. Wynn and I dressed for supper formation and left Reich sprawled on his bed. When we got back from supper, Wynn and I went about getting our room ready for Saturday Morning Inspection (SAMI) and even straightened out Reich's clothing locker, shined his shoes and cleaned his field gear. When we sat down at our desks to start studying for tomorrow's classes, Reich sprung from his bed, having experienced a "miraculous" recovery. Wynn and I instinctively responded by charging big Bob, driving him to the back of his cubicle, the three of us laughing uncontrollably all the while. They were both great roommates.

The Nazi Flag Episode

My dad had a business friend who had been one of Darby's Rangers in WWII. In the Fall of our Plebe year, Mister Langona visited West Point and presented me with a large Nazi flag. I have no idea what he expected me to do with it, but being only 17 years old, I thought it would be humorous to raise that flag on the North Area uniform flag before reveille. Those of you who were "minute callers" that morning might recall having seen it. At breakfast formation they asked who did it. I had to 'fess up to being the culprit as the flag belonged to Mr. Langona. After breakfast I was directed to take the elevator to the 6th floor of north barracks to report to our regimental TAC officer. The colonel was sitting behind his desk and the cadet regimental commander was standing at parade rest to the side. While I stood at rigid attention the colonel proceeded to tell me he had been a POW in WWII and what that flag represented. It was a lesson not to be forgotten.

Walking the Area

Every cadet was allowed a certain number of demerits each month. Every demerit over that quota resulted in an hour walking the area, which meant marching back and forth across the paved barrack's area with a rifle on your shoulder. You were allowed to switch the 9.5 pound rifle between left and right shoulder, and mercifully, there was a 10 minute break at the end of each hour.

My Nazi flag prank resulted in me receiving a slug of demerits which equated to me walking the area every Wednesday after class and every Saturday between lunch and supper formations, for 5 weeks.

My Worst Day

Every Saturday morning your room was subject to inspection (SAMI) and you had to stand inspection in ranks before the parade. These were two routine ways to collect demerits. When you were walking the area, you were subject to another inspection in rank at the start of the punishment tour. This was another source of demerits.

One Saturday, besides walking the area, I also had guard duty that night, and after supper was subject to yet another inspection in ranks before being dispatched to my assigned guard posts, which was in North Area barracks.

My uniform had come back from the tailors, and I failed to notice it still had chalk marks where it had been adjusted. I didn't have the opportunity to change uniforms as my other dress grey uniform was now at the tailors for the same alteration. I had stood three inspections in ranks and received demerits for the same infraction three times. Although I had walked off four hours, I now had more demerits than I had at the start of the day.

These were painful lessons. This "gross" Plebe wised up and I never had to walk the area again.

Football Highlights

Army vs Syracuse, November 5th. We played Syracuse in Yankee Stadium. Syracuse was a nationally ranked team, led by All-American running back Ernie Davis. Luckily, I had completed my punishment tours, as those poor souls still walking the area were excluded from the trip. The rest of us were bused to the Bronx.

We marched from the buses to the stadium in company formation.

As we approached the stadium, we could hear the West Point Band playing inside. We entered the stadium through a portal behind the visiting team bullpen. The moment our company marched onto the field the upperclassmen yelled, "Pick up the beat." They knew from previous Army-Navy games that, outside the stadium we had been marching in step with the echo.

The band was playing "This Is Our Country" as we took our position on the field. It was a thrilling moment and I felt enormously proud of being a member of the Long Grey Line. Syracuse was referred to as "The Orange Men." Every member of the Corps had been issued two oranges, which were carried clandestinely in the interior pockets of our overcoats. Before marching off, we dropped our two oranges on the field, leaving the field covered with trampled oranges. The Army defense held the "Orange Men" to two field goals and we won 9-6.

Following the game, we had until midnight to explore New York City on our own. While we were out enjoying ourselves, the convoy of buses had been repositioned from Yankee Stadium in the Bronx to the westside of Manhattan. As midnight approached, individual cadets, cadets in pairs and in small groups emerged from the dark side streets to join their company mates, gathering alongside their assigned buses. At midnight, we were told to get into formation for an inspection in ranks. Our cadet company commander called us to attention and reported "All present!" to our company TAC officer. Then the pair of them rapidly "trooped the line," one rank at a time, deliberately not making eye contact with those being inspected. This was not a time to be issuing demerits for minor infractions.

As each line was inspected, that line took one step forward to make space for the next line to be inspected. The only reason you would receive any demerits was if you were too inebriated to take the one step forward or were missing your hat or some other part of your uniform. It was not uncommon for an inebriated cadet to be propped up by his company mates standing to his left and right.

Army vs Navy, November 26

We were awakened at 3 AM for an early breakfast of steak and eggs, which the upperclassmen let us enjoy without any harassment or interference. After breakfast we changed into our dress grey uniforms with long overcoats and marched in the dark, downhill to the seldom used "West Point" train station, which was situated on the west bank of the Hudson River. Immediately north of the station, the train track tunneled under the Plain, but we were not headed north. We were southbound to Philadelphia.

About an hour before we reached Philadelphia, we were provided a box lunch consisting of a sandwich, an apple, and a fruit drink. When we arrived at our destination, I was surprised that we were not in downtown Philadelphia, but at a rail yard adjacent to the stadium.

We marched the short distance to the stadium, and on cue, marched on to the field, company by company, as it is always done. The game was hard fought, but Navy's running back Joe Bellino proved to be the difference and we lost 12-17.

My parents had driven to the game and we linked up afterwards. We went to dinner at a Polynesian restaurant which had a floor show. A Navy commander and I were escorted on to the stage to participate in one of the numbers. They put grass skirts on us and rolled up our pants to expose our legs.

After the show my parents drove me to the main Philadelphia train station, where our train was waiting to take us back to West Point. Before boarding the train, we stood inspection in ranks as we had in New York City, except this time it was conducted alongside a train. The drill was always the same.

Plebe Christmas

In those days, Plebes did not go home for Christmas, and we had the place to ourselves after the upperclassmen went home on Christmas leave. Some parents came up and stayed at the Hotel Thayer, which mine did for a couple of days. Guys that had "one and only" girlfriends from back home invited them to spend the week at West Point. The Hotel Thayer had a wing where the dates stayed in dorm-like rooms. Arrangements were made so that parents and girlfriends could eat Christmas Dinner and certain other meals with their cadet in Washington Hall. We had a late, casual reveille formation and formation for meals if we were not escorting our parents or a date.

With the upperclassmen gone, the Plebes constituted the equivalent of a platoon and one of us (not me) was designated to be in charge. Ironically, the person our TAC chose to be our leader failed to graduate with us four years later.

It snowed heavily that week and West Point looked like a picture postcard. I especially remember walking in the snow to the Catholic Chapel for Christmas Mass and embracing the serenity of the service. The decorations were dark green and dark red. The altar servers were classmates and I remember Barry McCafferty being one of them. Barry went on to distinguish himself in two ways: before graduating, walking more than 100 hours on the area, qualifying him for the "Century Club," and after graduation achieving the rank of four star General.

President Kennedy's Inauguration

January 1961: We took the train to Washington DC to march in President Kennedy's inaugural parade. It was cold and snowing as we marched from the station to our "jump off" point for the parade. We were ready to go at the prescribed time, but we had to stand there an extra hour, enduring the bad weather, while the new President and his entourage paused for lunch, alleged to be lobster rolls.

After that we were free until midnight when we had to be back at the train station, assembled for the trip back to West Point. I had a blind date with a girl who was a freshman at Marymount in DC. (She was the daughter of friends of my parents.) We went to one of the Inaugural Balls that was open to us.

4

Plebe Year, Second Semester

Second Semester Roommates

My second semester roommates were Norm Smith and Bill Cesarski. Norm was from Delaware and Bill was from New Jersey. Bill was a baseball player. Our room also was above the tunnel with the window facing the gym, but on a different floor from the one I shared with Reich and Wynn.

Second semester we were allowed to have a radio and musical instrument in our room. When my parents came up for Plebe Christmas, they brought my stereo, electric guitar and my baritone ukulele. We were only allowed one instrument per person, so Norm claimed possession of the uke.

Bill Cesarski excelled in academics, and as an upperclassman would wear stars on his collar indicating that he was in the top 5% of our class in academics. Bill's academic brilliance was obscured by his goofy personality. In spite of the fact that he was a "star man," Norm nicknamed him "Plumb Bob," which Norm explained was the dumbest tool in the toolbox.

There was a window seat above the radiator. Norm and I sometimes sat there after "Taps" with the only light in the room coming from the window. Before going to bed, the two of us would harmonize on one or two folk songs, with me accompanying us on my baritone ukulele. The study time between supper and Taps was too precious to waste playing the ukulele, and I could play the uke in the dark so that didn't matter. Five minutes of this and we were ready to hit the hay. Bill Cesarski was smarter than either of us and he was already asleep, having finished his studies well before Taps.

Study Time, Tatoo and Taps

Study time was from after supper until "Taps" which was at 11:00 PM weekday and Sunday nights. We were expected to go to bed after Taps, presumably to get adequate sleep before reveille at 5:50 AM the next morning.

A few minutes before 10:00 PM, buglers from the West Point Band positioned themselves in the sallyports facing North, South and Central Areas, and precisely at 10:00 PM, played Tatoo to signal there was one hour until Taps and lights out.

The bugle call reverberated through the sallyport tunnel, against the barracks that bounded the area, and against the surrounding mountains. This was my favorite bugle call. Some nights, the bugler would step forward from the sallyport and take a bow to his cadet audience, hanging out of their windows applauding him.

One hour later, at 11:00 PM the buglers played Taps which was a serene ending to the day.

Late Lights

If one of you was deficient in any subject, your room was authorized "late lights." If your lights were observed after Taps, the cadet guard would ask if your room was authorized "late lights," and he was required to write you up for demerits if your "late lights" were unauthorized. If you replied "Authorized!" and you were not, that was a lie and an honor violation resulting in your separation from the Corps.

Gloom Period

The West Point campus was strikingly beautiful and during football season and in the spring, the scene was further enhanced by the presence of young women visiting with friends or dating a cadet. Not so during "gloom period," the stretch of days between Christmas leave for the upperclassmen and spring.

During "gloom period" the sky was always grey and the girls were few and far between. It was always cold and often snowed. I remember standing in ranks for reveille formation. It was still dark and the wind was blowing snow into our faces. I can only imagine how that felt to our southern brethren. Most winter days we wore our grey, short overcoats, but sometimes it was so cold and windy that the unform for the day was our class jackets under parkas. The fact that we had lost to Navy in football only made "gloom period" worse.

On Call, Sir the Days

Ten minutes before every formation, we were "on call" to our Cow squad leader's room, where we stood at rigid attention, while he and his roommate continued getting dressed, all the while firing a steady barrage of questions at us. The most frequently asked question was, "Give us the days."

"Sir, today is Monday, February 13, 1961. There are 144 days until graduation and 292 days until Army beat the hell out of Navy in Football. The movie tonight is 'Butterfield 8," starring Elizabeth Taylor and Laurence Harvey. The officer of the day is Major Smith."

Once the Cow roommates were dressed, our uniforms, shoeshine, and haircuts were inspected, which was another opportunity to receive demerits. Our appearance at company formation would reflect on our squad leader.

Walking to the Hotel Thayer

In those days there was very little for Plebes to do on a Saturday night, other than go the movies. Besides hanging around with my roommates, I recall hanging around with classmates Wally Temple and Howie Wilson. After the Saturday night movie, we would walk to the Hotel Thayer for a milkshake. Although it was about a mile each way, and cold this time of year, we had nothing better to do.

Discovering Another Guitar Player

Walking back from the Saturday night movie, I could hear someone playing an electric guitar in his room. My hearing oriented me to the division of barracks, where I could see there was only one illuminated room on the floor where the sound was coming from.

I didn't know if the room belonged to a classmate or an upperclassman, but I boldly knocked on the door anyway, believing there is a special relationship between guitar players, regardless of their class.

As it turned out, the room belonged to one of our classmates, Jon Little, and the room was stuffed with other Plebes sitting on the beds, listening to him play. Jon's parents had given him a 1959-1960 golden Gibson Les Paul, which would become a classic. My guitar was an inexpensive knock off, which I had bought with caddying money my senior year of high school.

Discovering Jon, afforded me another destination for Saturday nights, and we spent many Saturday nights jamming. Jon was from Kentucky and into country blues which I, being from Long Island, had never heard. He taught me the Jimmy Reed riff.

The 100 Night Show

The "100 Night Show" is an annual event, produced and performed by the Firsties to celebrate there were only 100 days until their graduation. The play is a spoof of cadet life. The entire Corps attends the performance as do many of the officers on post and their wives. Some of the more recognizable officers in the academic and tactical departments are portrayed in the play, with their characterization being humorous exaggerations.

Recognition

The graduation parade for the class of 1961 was June 6th. Their graduation ceremony was the next day.

For the Class of 1964, the graduation parade was the second-to-last thing to be endured as Plebes. Following the parade, the companies marched from the Plain back to their area of barracks, as we normally did, but this time there was one more inspection in ranks. Actually, it was a mock inspection, with each upper classmen taking a quick turn at verbally abusing each Plebe one more time. Some squad leaders smashed their rifle butt against the breast plates of the Plebes in their squad, as a way of acknowledging the toughness their squad members had demonstrated through the course of the year. After a short while, the upperclassmen lined up and each shook hands with each of us, congratulating us on having successfully completed our Plebe year. The handshake symbolized recognition and recognition was reserved for this moment.

5

Yearling Year Summer Training

Camp Buckner, July-August 1961

When we returned to West Point from 30-day leave, we had to sign back into our cadet companies and gather our field gear which was stored in the basement of our company barracks. Army trucks were already waiting outside our barracks to transport us to Camp Buckner for our Yearling year field training.

Camp Buckner is located about 15 miles northwest of West Point. At Camp Buckner we were housed in pre-fab aluminum barracks, which were designed to house about 60 soldiers - or 60 cadets in our case. Each barracks was a single-story affair on a cement slab. We slept in double-decked steel-framed beds. The latrine, sinks and showers were in the middle, so half the group was bunked in the front of the sinks and half bunked to the rear.

The mess hall was a large single-story, wooden building with window screens instead of glass windows. (Picture a Boy Scout camp dining hall.) Casual dances then called "hops" were scheduled on the weekends and the mess hall served as a dancing pavilion. Dates could be arranged through the Cadet Hostess and the girls stayed in a guest house that was near the mess hall. I have no idea how they got there.

The field training was very interesting and varied, and I found myself enjoying soldiering, doing well, and identifying myself as a soldier.

One of the first activities was to requalify on the rifle range with newly issued M-14 rifles. We then received hands-on training from officers, NCOs and enlisted men from the five combat arms:

- Infantry - Firing M60 machine guns, 81mm mortars, and 3.5" rocket launchers
- Artillery - fire direction center procedures, and firing 105 mm howitzers
- Armor - driving M60 tanks and firing the main gun
- Engineers - Using C-4 explosives to blow up bunkers, and erecting a Baily bridge over the lake
- Signal - Correct radio procedure, using man-packed PRC-10 radios, and erecting RC292 antennas

We conducted platoon and company maneuvers involving offensive and defensive tactics.

We received one week of Recondo training, which was a compressed Ranger experience (hand-to-hand combat, rappelling, "slide for life," and day and night patrolling.) On one patrol we were inserted from an H-21 banana shaped helicopter. We were deliberately deprived of sleep that week and I remember struggling to stay awake on that patrol, in and out of consciousness as we progressed to our objective.

On the weekends Kenny Waldrop, Dick Knight, Alex Hottell and I started jamming in the "sinks" of our barracks. Kenny played bass, Dick played drums, Alec was the lead guitar and I played rhythm guitar. After a couple of weeks of this, our classmates requested that we play for that week's "hop" and we played every weekend hop for the rest of the summer.

With our summer training completed, we returned to West Point a few days before Labor Day weekend.

6

Yearling Year First Semester (Fall 1961)

Roommates

For my second year in Company H-2, my first semester roommates were Bob Reich (again) and Doug Alitz who was a "turnback" from the class of 1963. Doug was a wrestler and his dad both coached the intercollegiate wrestling team and taught all of us wrestling plebe year.

In the fall I dated high school girl friends Ceil O'Regan and Carolyn Zimmerman. Doug's girlfriend Janie's father was a colonel and doctor at the West Point Hospital. Janie occasionally invited us to her house, and I remember my date being Carolyn. Once inside Janie's house, we replaced our roman-collared grey tunic tops with more comfortable crew-neck sweaters, which we had purchased from the PX for such occasions. Candles provided the lighting as we listened to Johnny Mathis music. Doug and Janie would get married but later divorced.

Academics

In academics we had another full boat with calculus II, differential equations, probability and statistics, Spanish II, chemistry, history of the United States, history of modern Europe and Asia, comparative literature, psychology, physical training, and military heritage.

Football Highlights

The football highlight was beating Penn State 10-6 at Penn State. Since Joe Bellino had graduated, we thought we would have a good shot at Navy. That was not to be the case. Navy won for a second year in a row 13-7.

Jamming in the "Sinks"

Company H-2 was located in North Area near the gym. Each barracks had four floors with four rooms and a shared bathroom/shower on each floor. The basements of the barracks were referred to as "the sinks" and that was where we had our gym lockers. A pay phone and a Coke machine were also located there, so on weekends there was usually a handful of people there waiting to use the pay phone or to get a Coke.

On Saturday nights Ken, Dick and I gathered to "jam" in 'the "sinks." Alex Hottell was frequently on field trips with the swim team, glee club or lightweight football team so he rarely participated.

An unusual aspect of the "sinks" was that they were connected under the barracks so you could visit someone in another barracks without having to go outside. Because of the interconnectivity of the sinks, each weekend more and more cadets would gather to witness our jam sessions, which were joined by Tim Sanchez (Class of 1963) and Tom Culver (Class of 1962). Tim was an excellent blues and R&B guitarist and Tom was a very good R&B singer. After maybe three weekends of this, the gathered audience picked up our gear and escorted us to the Weapons Room where we would play every weekend thereafter for the next 3 years.

Initially we were banned from playing "The Twist" but the cadet corporal of the guard kept an eye on the door to give us early warning. One night Mrs. Westmoreland, the Superintendent's wife, suddenly materialized, outflanking the surprised and nervous guard. She signaled for the band to keep playing and even did the twist with a couple of upperclassmen. From that moment on "The Twist" was officially considered appropriate for cadets.

7

Yearling Year, Second Semester

Second Semester Roommate

My second semester roommate was Larry Strickland. Larry was from California, so I invited him to spend spring break with me on Long Island. I made a date with a girl I had met the previous summer and she fixed Larry up with one of her girlfriends. We went to a rock-n-roll bar in West Hempstead that had a band I had witnessed the previous summer. The band was the "Fortunes," but not the British band of the same name.

Assistant Lacrosse Manager

Bill, Cauthen, (Class of 1962) was the senior manager of the lacrosse team and he recruited me to be his assistant. Bill knew me as he had roomed with my Plebe year squad leader. Midway through the season defenseman Bobby Hancock broke his hand. His hand was in a cast and he was unable to practice with the rest of the team on the field. He took me aside and started teaching me offensive moves so that he could practice defense against me. He told me I had good potential and should go out for the team next year. The possibility of that had never crossed my mind, but the seed was planted.

General MacArthur's Speech, May 12, 1962

MacArthur had graduated #1 in the class of 1903, distinguished himself in WWI combat, and had served as West Point's Superintendent from 1919-1922. While Superintendent, he had modernized the curriculum, instated off-site summer training, and intramural sports for all cadets.

May 12, 1962. We were not pleased that it was mandatory to attend Saturday lunch to witness General MacArthur receiving the Thayer Award. As he started to speak, you could still hear the clanging of silverware as some cadets were still trying to finish their desert.

"This morning as I was leaving the hotel, a doorman asked, 'And where are you bound for today general?' To which I replied [emphatically] 'West Point!' He said, 'A beautiful place. Have you ever been there before?' At that point the Corps erupted with applause. The clanging of the silverware ceased, and you could hear a pin drop in the immensity of Washington Hall. We realized we were witnessing something historic.

He continued. "Duty, Honor, Country. Those three hallowed words reverently dictate what you ought to be, what you can be; what you will be. ... They mold you for your future roles as custodians of the nation's defense. ... And what sort of soldiers are those you are to lead? Are they reliable? Are they brave? Are they capable of victory? ... When I think of his patience under adversity, of his courage under fire, and of his modesty in victory, I am filled with an emotion of admiration I cannot put into words. ... The soldier, above all other men, is required to practice the greatest act of religious training: sacrifice. ... You now face a new world, a world of change. ... And through all this welter of change and development your mission remains fixed, determined, inviolable. It is to win our wars."

He ended with, "And when I cross the river for the last time, my final thoughts will be of the Corps, the Corps and the Corps."

Me (left) and Doug Bennett, Plebe Year, fall 1960

Mom and Dad with me after a parade Cow Year, Fall 1962

42 | SIR, THE DAYS!

Joan and I after my Graduation," June 3, 1964

8

Cow Year Summer Training – Beast Barracks Revisited

Cow Year Class Trip, June 1962

The class of 1962 graduated on June 6 and the next day we were new "Cows" and off on our Cow year class trip.

We were bused to Stewart Air Force Base where fighter aircraft were put on display for us, and we were given presentations on the roles and capabilities of the U.S. Air Force. In those days 5% of our class were allowed to go into the Air Force and this was their opportunity to recruit from our class.

Our trip took us to New London CT, where we visited the U.S Coast Guard Academy, and also visited the U.S. Navy Submarine School, where we observed training and got to board a docked, active-duty submarine. Above deck, everything was very formal, formally saluting the flag and the Officer on Deck. Below deck, it was just the opposite. The crew donned tee shirt, shorts and shower shoes (flip flops), which I imagined was an accommodation for what would be a long cruise in very tight quarters.

From there we attended the Army Signal School at Fort Monmouth NJ and the Engineer School at Fort Belvoir VA. In each instance we were lectured on the roles and capabilities of those branches, given demonstrations and given some hands-on training on certain items of equipment. They put on quite a show, obviously trying to impress us to go into that branch when we graduated.

Upon returning to West Point, classmates scheduled for summer training in August would go home on 30-day leave, while those of us who were scheduled for "First Beast" detail in July would stay at West Point, to train and practice for our upcoming assignment. Our 30-day leave would come in August.

"Beast Barracks" Revisited, July 1962

July 1962: I was a "First Beast" squad leader. I had 8 "new cadets" assigned to my squad and I was responsible for the first 4 weeks of their training. This was part of our leadership training and development, and it was an extremely intense experience.

My roommate was the squad leader for another squad and the usual practice was for the two squads to be trained together. We had to prepare a lesson plan for each hour of training, conduct the training, and then rate each of our 8 squad members on each block of training at the end of the day. Our training day ended at 2130 (9:30 PM). After that it was time to rate each of our squad members on that day's training, and then to prepare the lesson plans for the next day. I would prepare half of the lesson plans and my roommate would prepare the other half. I would be the instructor for the lessons I had prepared, and my roommate would be the demonstrator and provide individual instruction for anyone having difficulty with the lesson. Our roles would be reversed for the lesson plans he prepared.

I had a new cadet named Doug Sims. He was from Mississippi and not unlike Gomer Pyle. He was thinking and moving at about 30 MPH when everyone else was operating at 100 MPH, but he obviously really wanted to be a cadet. Our platoon leader started to single him out for admonition. I privately confronted the platoon leader and told him Sims was my responsibility and he should back off. I was tough on Sims but I challenged him in increasing doses that I thought he could handle. By the end of "first beast" he was operating at 100 MPH like the others. All 8 of my new cadets graduated and Doug Sims graduated as a cadet captain.

As I mentioned, this was an extremely intense experience and each of the upperclassmen were granted one 30-hour pass at some point to break the tension. The pass was good from noon on Saturday until supper formation, 6 pm Sunday. The squad leaders who roomed together could not take the same weekend, as one had to cover for the other. I think I took my break between weeks 3 and 4.

I took the bus from West Point to New York City, and the Long Island Railroad from there. I didn't have a date, nor any plans for Saturday night. I just wanted to get away from the pressure and intensity of being a "Beast Barracks" squad leader.

Sunday morning I attended Catholic Mass with my parents. At that time, a new parish was being formed, and while the church was being built, Sunday Mass was held in a basement room underneath Gertz shopping center. The room was called "The Lions Den." Communion time, I happened to observe a strikingly beautiful girl going up to Communion and caught another glimpse of her as she returned to her seat. She was relatively tall, had dark hair, and had radiant blue eyes. I remember wishing that I had the opportunity to meet a girl like that, but realized that was not going to happen with me being a "Beast

Barracks" squad leader at West Point. After lunch my parents drove me back to West Point; back to "Beast Barracks."

Long Island Lacrosse Club

Before going home on 30-day summer leave, I signed out for a stick, gloves, pads and a helmet, from our equipment room. I contacted the Long Island Lacrosse Club so I could I join their summer lacrosse league when I got home. The team I was assigned to was sponsored by a bar in Sea Cliff, which happened to be a C.W. Post College hangout. Aside from me, all the other member of our team had been teammates at either C.W. Post or Rutgers, and all were experienced college players. I was not.

Every day I went to Hicksville High School, ran 2 miles, played "wall ball" for an hour on the handball court, practiced shooting at an empty net, and practiced scooping by chasing after my missed shots. The team practiced on Thursday nights. That was the extent of my training. We played double-headers on Sundays at Jones Beach Park, so I got to play in 8 games before returning to West Point. That was the extent of my playing experience.

9

Cow Year, First Semester

Reorganization Week

When we returned to West Point from summer duty or 30-day leave, we discovered that all of us Cows had been reassigned to different cadet companies. I was no longer in Company H-2. Now I was in B-2. Mike Goff and Larry Strickland also moved from H-2 to B-2. Everyone else came from some other cadet company. My assigned roommate was Gwynn Vaughn who was a wrestler and offensive guard on the football team. Gwynn was very religious and attended bible study every morning before reveille.

The Inmates

With Tim Sanchez and Tom Culver having graduated, our jam band needed another lead guitarist and a singer. Our bass player, Ken Waldrop, was also reassigned to Company B-2 and he discovered that one of our Plebes, Steve Singer, played the guitar and played well. Although just a Plebe, Steve would become our new lead guitarist. Ken was his big brother and no one seemed to mind that we had a Plebe playing with us in the Weapons Room. Tom Culver was irreplaceable as the lead singer, so we simply shared those duties. If you knew the words to the song, you were the lead on that song. The band finally decided on a name which was "The Inmates," which had a double meaning.

Cow Year Academics

Cow year had the reputation of being the toughest academic year, and it lived up to its reputation. It was very heavy on engineering. Our classes were: thermodynamics, solid and fluid mechanics, electricity and electronics, economics, civil and military law, U.S government, physical education, and military history.

I struggled with thermodynamics, and I blame our instructor for that. Early on I asked him what was the difference between entropy and enthalpy? He blew me off with "It is the measure of energy in the universe" and continued with the lesson he was presenting. He could have seen me after class, but he didn't. From day one I didn't understand what this course was about and was failing the entire fall semester. When I was home on Christmas leave, my father paid a Grumman Aerospace engineer to tutor me on his lunch hours. We did a chapter a day, using my textbook, starting with Chapter 1. He turned the lights on for me. When I returned to West Point, I maxed the final exam. I am sure they checked my paper to see if I had cheated (which I hadn't). The difference was that I was tutored by someone who could explain it to me. Beyond learning something about thermodynamics, I learned a more valuable lesson, which was to take into consideration where the student (or other person) is coming from and explain things in a way they can relate to.

Company B-2: Intramural Football

Unless you were on an in-season intercollegiate team, you had to play an intramural sport each season.

There were several sports for each season, and the Firsties (seniors) of the company decided who would be on each team. As Cows (juniors) we were able to provide input into this process, and I voiced that I wanted to play football, and so it would be.

In those days intramural football was 8- man tackle with 3 backs and 5 linemen. The competition between companies was pretty fierce. Many of the players had played high school football but just were not big enough or good enough to play at the intercollegiate level. To prevent total domination by these players in intramurals, you could only play a particular sport twice. It was my first time playing organized tackle football and I loved it. I played middle linebacker, offensive guard and sometime ran back punts. In spite of breaking my thumb and one of my fingers, I loved it and managed to play a second season of intramural football as a Firstie.

October 1962: The Cuban Missile Crisis

Communist revolutionary Fidel Castro seized power in Cuba in 1959. In response to this, the CIA trained 1,400 Cuban exiles to invade Cuba, with the goal of overthrowing Castro. The invasion occurred at the Bay of Pigs in April, 1961, but it was repelled at the beachhead without the CIA's promised support.

It was at the height of the "Cold War" and the Soviet Union was eager to support their communist ally, Fidel, against the U.S.

On October 22, 1962, President Kennedy went on TV to report to the American people that a week earlier, a U-2 spy plane had confirmed that the Soviet Union was installing ballistic missile sites in Cuba with nuclear warheads capable of destroying U.S. cities as far north as Boston and as far west as Salt Lake City.

After supper we were assembled in Thayer Hall theater and briefed on the dire DEFCON-2 situation. Several times during the night I woke up and looked out our window (which faced north overlooking the Plain), expecting to see an orange glow in the sky, which would have indicated that New York City, 50 miles to our south, had been destroyed. That did not happen.

President Kennedy imposed a naval blockade against Cuba and the Russians supply ships turned away, thereby averting a nuclear world war. The missiles were removed from Cuba in exchange for our missiles being removed from Turkey.

Army Football Highlights

The second game of the season was against Syracuse, this time with Floyd Little. The game was played at the now defunct Polo Grounds, in upper Manhattan. We won 9-2. After the game, former roommate, Bob Wynn, and I hung out together, searching for an inexpensive place to eat. (Bob and I were now in different cadet companies). As we approached Times Square, Tad's Steakhouse came into view, and Tad's would meet our monetary criteria.

The team played the University of Michigan in Ann Arbor, and we watched on a wide screen set up in the Army Theater. Our Army team was outclassed, and we lost 7-17.

Our next game was against Penn State, played at home in West Point's Miche Stadium. Army won 9-6. Many of our classmates on the football team came from Pennsylvania and they got very fired up playing against Penn State. Paul Deitzel was our new head coach and he designated our defensive players as the "Chinese Bandits," which is something he had done at LSU.

Our second trip of the season was to Washington D.C. to play George Washington University, which we beat 14-10. We had the evening off, and I went to the Showboat Lounge, where legendary guitarist Charlie Bird regularly played.

Army-Navy Game, December 1, 1962

There was a sophomore ("Youngster" in Annapolis jargon) on the Navy squad named Roger Staubach, who at the beginning of the season was the third-string quarterback. As the season progressed, the players ahead of him were injured and by the Army-Navy game Roger was the starter. We had not been paying enough attention to what this guy could do in a game situation. I don't think the Navy coaches were even aware of what this guy could do in a game. He probably didn't throw the ball any better in practice than the two quarterbacks ahead of him. He was a great athlete and natural leader who did astounding things in games. One second he was there; the next second he was someplace else. Navy won 34-14.

Company B-2: intramural Wrestling

My winter intramural sport was wrestling, and I turned out to be a pretty good wrestler. I had very good upper body strength and I won all but one of my bouts. The bout I lost was against a Firstie who was from Hawaii. He had wrestled in high school, and he knew how to use his legs as a weapon. He tied me up like a pretzel. After the season was over, I bumped into him at the gym and asked him to teach me how to use my legs, which he graciously did. I would wrestle again as a Firstie and this time I would go undefeated.

10

Cow Year, Second Semester

Exchange Week at Annapolis

Cow year, every member of the class would spend one week at the U.S Naval Academy. You would room with a midshipman whose roommate was at West Point, staying with your cadet roommate.

You would stand formation with your naval counterpart, eat at his table, and attend classes with him. The academic classes were virtually the same, although their engineering was more oriented towards shipboard matters, such as propulsion engineering. As would be expected, their study of military history went into more detail on the naval contributions to the overall war effort. Naval tactics class was a whole different thing.

At West Point, our formations were held outside, and we marched down the street to Washington Hall for meals. At Annapolis, their formations were in the hallways of Bancroft Hall, and they marched down the hallway to the dining area, which was part of Bancroft Hall. I assume the difference was deliberate as onboard ships they would be in enclosed environments.

Sunday, I attended Mass at the Naval Academy Chapel, which was used for both Catholic and Protestant services. It was very impressive, as is the Cadet Chapel at West Point. I was very moved by the singing of the Navy Hymn at the end of Mass.

> Eternal Father, strong to save,
> Whose arm hath bound the restless wave,
> Who bidd'st the mighty ocean deep
> Its own appointed limits keep;
> Oh, hear us when we cry to Thee,
> For those in peril on the sea!

Spring 1963: Army Lacrosse

Before training began for the 1963 lacrosse season, I asked Coach Adams if I could go out for the team and he encouraged me to do that. (Recall my only experience was having played 8 games in the Long Island Lacrosse Club's summer league.)

I was not experienced or skilled enough to be an attacker, nor big enough to be a defender so I was destined to be a midfielder. I did have better than average endurance and speed, but I lacked experience. My classmates who had joined the program as Plebes had two years more experience than I did. I did make the B squad (JV) team and "played up" a couple of games on A squad as a third-string middie. I loved playing the game. My only regret in life was that I did not go out for the team a year earlier, as a Yearling. I could have handled that. I knew it would have been too much for me as a Plebe.

Spring Break 1963

My cousin Chris was a sophomore at St. John's and I asked her to fix me up with a date for the upcoming Armed Forces Day weekend. My only stipulation was that my date had to live close, meaning not Brooklyn, Queens or the Bronx. Chris described a girl who was a freshman on her basketball teammate, who Chris believed might even be in our same parish. From Chris' description I wondered if it could be the same girl I had seen the previous summer. Unbeknownst to me, my father noticed this girl at Sunday Mass months later, and after Mass spotted a friend of mine who happened to be a high school classmate of this girl. My dad learned her name was Joan Flanagan and he called the only Flanagan family listed in Jericho. Joan's mother answered the phone, and recognizing my father's name, revealed that she was the former Bea Makofske from Uniondale where their families had grown up together. After catching up on old times, her mom put Joan on the phone and the date was arranged.

In those days each cadet company had only one telephone and it was in the company orderly room. That night I was called to the orderly room where my dad was on the phone, which was extremely unusual as that phone was only used for official business. When I phoned my family it was from a pay phone which was located in the basement of the barracks. My dad told me he had arranged a date for me for Armed Forces weekend. When I told him Cousin Chris was fixing me up, he told me "This girl is a knockout. Break it!" I was disappointed because I had hopes that the girl Chris was fixing me up with was the girl I had seen at Mass the previous summer, but as it turns out, Cousin Chris actually had forgotten about my request.

Armed Forces Day Weekend, May 1963

When I was going to pick up my blind date, my dad wanted me to take his Buick Rivera to impress her, but I elected to take my mother's Studebaker Lark for the opposite reason. I wanted her to like me; not my father's car.

When I went to pick up my blind date, the girl who opened the door was the same girl I had spotted in church the previous summer. It was Joan.

Joan was unlike any girl I knew or would ever date. She was beautiful, smart and her blue eyes radiated positive energy, besides which, she was from the same roots - an Irish Catholic girl from Long Island.

Friday night we went to a movie in Glen Cove and had pizza afterwards. The next day we played Hofstra in lacrosse and Joan had to work.

Saturday night I took Joan to dinner at the Top of the Sixes, a restaurant I had heard about. After dinner, we went to the Gaslight East, which was located on East 156th Street. It was an exclusive key club, which my dad had recommended, and he had a key. The club's motif was that of a "roaring twenties speakeasy." When you knocked on the door you had to say "Joe sent me" for the door to be opened. Once inside you had to show the doorman your key. The footprint of the club was small and cozy, but it had four floors with different entertainment on each floor. One floor we visited was a piano bar, and the other had a dixieland band. (I learned later that the club closed in 1971.)

On the way home the Studebaker Lark was misbehaving. We both laughed as the car backfired as we were driving through the Lincoln Tunnel. By the time we got to Joan's neighborhood, it was well after 3 AM. I turned off the car lights as I turned onto Joan's street so as to not wake up her parents or the neighbors. Our clandestine arrival was foiled, however, as the car backfired one more time and all the house lights on the street lit up.

June Week 1963

I invited Joan to West Point for 1963 June Week. I don't recall that I gave a lot of thought about the logistics involved. As it turned out, she drove herself to West Point, using her parent's 1962 Mercury Comet. This was a pretty courageous endeavor for a young girl at that time, given the distance and the reliability of their car. Decades later I learned that the car had broken down enroute and had to be repaired in a local gas station before she arrived at West Point.

My fondest memory of that June Week was slow dancing at the First Class Club. During June Week the First Class Club was surrendered to the Cows (junior) class, as the graduating Firsties had better things to do. The First Class Club was just over the hill on the north end of the Plain. It was a stone hewed building surrounded by a high stone wall, with the only entrance being an archway gate through the wall. It was very cozy and romantic. It had been re-purposed and remodeled from the century-old ammunition storage magazine.

The "Black Eye" Speech

After three years as Superintendent, General Westmoreland (Class of 1936) was being assigned to command the 18th Airborne Corps. One night, between the graduation of the Class of 1963 and our First Class trip, a half dozen of us from Company B-2 were standing around the barracks front stoops waiting for others to join us before going to the movies. While we were standing there talking, a lone figure came jogging down the road towards us in the dusk. Nobody paid any attention to the jogger until it was too late. The jogger turned out to be none other than General Westmoreland returning from playing tennis. He had gone out of his way to come over to say goodbye to us. From his perspective, we didn't even salute him in return. In truth, we just didn't recognize him in the near darkness. In his eyes, we were totally lacking in military courtesy, and he had failed in his mission to instill that in us. He was so disappointed he assembled the whole class in Thayer Hall auditorium to air his feelings. He wondered out loud if he had failed in his mission to inspire in us the spirit and tradition of the Army and the Long Grey Line. This was his last-ditch attempt. This would become known as our "black eye speech".

11

First Class Year, Summer 1963

First Class Trip, June 1963

The day after the Class of 1963 graduated, Army buses were positioned outside our barracks to take us to Stewart Air Base from where we would embark on our First-Class trip. The two-week trip would take us to Ft. Benning for Infantry, Ft. Sill for Field Artillery and Ft. Bliss for Air Defense Artillery.

When we emerged from the barracks that morning, across the street were Joan, Jean and Sally, there to see us off. This was totally unexpected by us and obviously the three girls had decided to do this after they checked out from the hotel that morning. (Jean would marry Ed Sims and Sally would marry Larry Strickland after our graduation.)

On the plane ride to Fort Benning I wrote the first song I would ever write, inspired by my extended June Week date with Joan and the girls' unexpected send off. The song was "Parting Is Such Sweet Sorrow."

The Infantry School did not try to coddle us to the degree the other branch schools did and would do.

The Infantry School did give us lectures and demonstrations as did the other branch schools, but the emphasis was more on hands-on training, and us getting dirty. In battle the last 100 yards belonged to the infantry and they were proud of it.

Our next stops were Fort Sill, Oklahoma for field artillery, Fort Bliss for air defense and rocket artillery, and the Armor School at Fort Knox, Kentucky. From there it was back to West Point, and for me, the beginning of my 30-day leave.

Summer Leave, July 1963

My 30-day leave began when we got back to West Point from our class trip. When I came home, I was very disappointed to discover that Joan had a new boyfriend, Chuck, the lifeguard.

While home on leave, I attended a party with my sister Barbara and brother-in-law Jim. At the party I met Sherry DePalma who was there with her older sister. We dated until I departed for advanced infantry training with a mechanized infantry battalion in Germany.

12

First Class Summer Training – Manheim, Germany

World War II and Post-War Berlin

World War II ended in Europe when Germany surrendered in May 1945. By early 1945 it was obvious that Germany would be defeated and in February Joseph Stalin, Winston Churchill and President Franklin Roosevelt met in Yalta to determine how to occupy post-war Germany. Germany was to be divided into four occupation zones with the Russian zone extending as far west as the Elbe River, and the British, French and American zones being west of the Elbe River. Berlin would be in the Russian zone as it is 200 miles east of the Elbe River.

Given the Yalta agreement, General Eisenhower was intent that no American or British lives should be expended in a climactic battle for Berlin, only to have to turn Berlin over to the Russians. The battle of Berlin was waged solely by the vengeful Russians who would crush the last remnants of the Nazi regime, but it cost them 100,000 Russian soldiers killed in the battle.

Under the terms of the Yalta agreement, Berlin itself would be divided into four zones with each party guaranteed access to each-others' zones, provided the visitors were in uniform, ostensibly so they could be kept under observation. In June 1948, the Soviets tried to deny the allies access to Berlin. This resulted in the "Berlin Airlift" which supplied the Berliners for eleven months until the Russian ceased their choke hold on Berlin. There was another crisis in 1961. This time the Soviets built the Berlin Wall to deny the free flow of traffic between the zones. In order to exercise the terms of the Yalta agreement, the American Army continued to dispatch a uniformed patrol each day through Check Point Charlie into east Germany. It was always a tense situation with armed Russian and east German soldiers checking the vehicles' paperwork and occupants.

Berlin, August 1963

Only about a quarter of the class of 1964 was assigned to AIT (advanced infantry training) in Germany in August 1963. Some had done their AIT the previous year and others did their AIT in July of this year.

We were flown to Frankfurt, Germany, where we immediately boarded U.S Air Force cargo planes that flew us to Berlin through a narrow air corridor, provided under the terms of the Yalta agreement.

When we landed at Tempelhof Airport we were subjected to a short briefing, after which we would have the afternoon and evening free to sightsee Berlin on our own. The gist of the briefing it was that we were under orders to stay in uniform and advised to go easy on the German beer as it was stronger than we were used to. We were each issued a card which indicated our official status and provided us with a phone number to call should we get into a jam with local or other military authorities. We all obeyed the order to stay in uniform but the guys I was hanging with did not heed the advice. We spent the entire night barhopping and sampling the beer in each place.

Hundreds of us were to be billeted in a gymnasium filled with double-deck army bunks. Many of us elected to spend the night sampling Berlin bars and beers rather than return to the gym to get some shut-eye. That morning we were scheduled to be bused through Checkpoint Charlie, in uniform and on an olive-drab bus clearly marked "U.S. Army." We got back to the gym on time, but I was feeling the ill effects of too much beer and no sleep. To miss the formation would be a court martial offense for "missing movement," which was only one notch lower than an AWOL (absent without leave) offense. I had no choice but to be present at the morning roll call formation. I skipped breakfast as I was too sick to eat. After breakfast time, we boarded the buses and headed to Checkpoint Charlie, which would be our gateway to east Germany. I sat on the right side of the last seat of the bus, so I could hang my head out the window to get some fresh air. I was struggling to not throw up on the bus, which would have resulted in a boat load of demerits for me when I got back to West Point, for "bringing dishonor on the Corps of Cadets and the U.S. Army."

At Checkpoint Charlie our bus was stopped, as was the normal procedure, while the driver provided the armed guards with the paperwork. While this was going on a young Russian (or east German) soldier was pacing alongside our bus, trying to look tough with his submachine gun slung over his shoulder. When he got to the rear of the bus his eyes met mine and he broke down laughing.

There was a vacant lot to the right of Checkpoint Charlie. This was where the Russians had found Hitler's charred body and they felt no obligation to improve this area. As we got rolling again, I looked back towards the Berlin Wall and noticed that all the buildings on the

Russian side of the wall were unimproved remnants of World War II. The side of the buildings facing west Berlin had been fixed up. It was a charade. One of the sites that we were taken to was a cemetery where the 100,000 Russian soldiers who died in the Berlin battle were buried in a mass grave. There was an enormous statue overlooking the site.

August 1963, Coleman Kaserne, Mannheim, Germany

For the month of August, I was assigned to a mechanized infantry company, situated at Coleman Kaserne (barracks), which had been home for a German battalion in World War II. In our West Point studies, WWII seemed as ancient as the American Civil War. But yet, here it was only 18 years later and there were still bullet pock marks on the barracks walls.

Coleman Barracks was located near Mannheim, Germany. The 2nd Battalion 9th Infantry had recently rotated to Germany from the 2nd Infantry Division at Fort Benning. I filled a temporary vacancy, as an acting platoon leader. The enlisted people were told to treat me as a third lieutenant. Of course there is no such rank, but it established my authority to be somewhat like a warrant officer. My radio operator's name was Dennis Carden. In spite of being a two-year draftee, as were many of the soldiers during the Cold War, Carden took his soldiering seriously and did a great job. We got along great, and he was my link to the other members of the platoon.

I remember doing PT and running every morning, giving and receiving classes on individual soldiering skills, and performing first echelon maintenance chores on our M113 APCs (armored personnel carriers), which were located in the motor pool, a quarter mile from the company barracks. This was during the Cold War, and during my time there, we had two alerts which required all officers and men to be assembled at some odd nighttime hour, draw weapons and ammunition, and drive our APCs in the dark to a pre-determined site where we were to defend against a Soviet Russian invasion.

One night every man in the company had to traverse a multi-leg compass course through a growth forest, thick with young coniferous trees. As I emerged from the forest at the end of the last leg of the course, there waiting for us was our company commander. My first reaction was to be thankful that I did not embarrass myself or West Point, and then to be pleased with myself that I finished at the head of my platoon. As I stood alongside our CO, one by one the members of my platoon emerged from the forest, each having successfully navigated the course. I was proud of them. The leadership principle was once again reinforced. Their collective success was more important than my individual success.

I was living in a BOQ (bachelor officer quarters) where most of the young officers of our battalion were housed. After duty hours and on weekends we took a cab to Mannheim for entertainment, where we mostly frequented a bar called The Satellite Club. From outside the club, you could hear loud rock music emanating from inside. Once inside, I immediately checked out the band which had matching white Fender equipment. The very first song I heard was Chuck Berry's "Sweet Little Sixteen" which blew me away. Here I was in the heart of Germany and I'm hearing "Sweet Little Sixteen" being sung in English!

In place of a cash cover charge, you had to buy a shot of cognac with your first beer. For us the cognac tasted like kerosene, so we all dumped it into our first beer, which got the evening underway in a hurry.

The Field Training Exercise, and Unit Evaluation, Baumholder, Germany

It just so happened that our battalion was scheduled for its annual field training exercise and evaluation during my tenure as a "third lieutenant." In spite of the fact that the performance of my platoon would reflect directly on our company commander, he did not replace me with a real lieutenant for the exercise.

The FTX was conducted in Baumholder. We were awakened in the middle of the night and had to drive our APCs to a railroad loading dock, someplace not too far from Coleman Kaserne. At daybreak the APCs were driven onto flat cars, each starting at the rear of the train and moving forward over multiple cars until it was positioned on its destined car, with two APCS on each flat car. Once all the APCS were in place and properly fastened to their flat car, we retreated to passenger cars where we all promptly fell asleep.

When we arrived, we had to unload the APCs one-by-one in the reverse order we loaded them up. It was a long day's journey to get to the Baumholder maneuver area, with the convoy proceeding in single file all the way. Enroute, we convoyed through the narrow winding streets of a Bavarian town. Daytime turned into nighttime. My position was in the commander's cupola of the first APC of my platoon. In the dim red light of the cupola I could follow our progress on a map which I had propped up in front of me. Following the dimmed taillights of the APC ahead of my platoon was monotonous and after 24 hours without sleep, I dosed off for just a second. When I looked up there was no APCs in front of me. The battalion had come to a fork in the road and all the APCs before me went one way and I and everyone behind me was following me the other way. It was very obvious where the break in the chain had occurred. I could only imagine what punishment might befall me, screwing up during the height of the Cold War. I had to turn my APC around and drive the entire length of the column behind me, and each of them had to turn around and follow me. I caught up to the rest of the battalion in their Baumholder assembly area. I was not court martialed, but subject to the chiding of the lieutenants of my company. I did very well in the field training exercise and my platoon passed its test.

13

First Class Year, First Semester

Ring Weekend, September 1963

Each West Point class determines its own motto and unique emblem. On a West Point ring, the class emblem is on one side of the ring and the West Point emblem, the helmet of Pallas Athena, is on the other side. Around the stone are the words "Duty Honor, Country" which is the West Point motto.

The first milestone of our First-Class year was receiving our West Point class rings. The ceremony was held in Cullum Hall. We were called forward by company to be presented our rings. As first classmen we were authorized to wear our rings. West Point rings are worn on the left hand. Before graduation, the ring is worn with the class emblem closest to our hearts. After graduation, the ring is worn with the West Point emblem closest to our hearts. That weekend was the "Ring Dance" and I invited Sherry DePalma to West Point for the weekend.

Academics

Structural analysis and design, propulsion engineering, ballistics engineering, literature and exposition, contemporary foreign governments, international relations, history of the military art, military psychology and leadership, responsibilities of junior officers, and physical training. Electives in management engineering and advanced electronics.

I signed up for an advanced electronics course. I had built a Heathkit radio and designed and built my own guitar reverb unit. I liked electronics and thought I might go into the Signal Corps. The prof who was going to teach the class advised me I might have trouble with this class. I persisted. The first day of class I noticed that I had not been in one class with any of the other guys. They were all first section types and I was not. That same day the prof started talking about Laplace transforms. I had no idea what he was talking about – and still don't. Since it was last semester and an elective, he gave me a 2.0 for showing up. I ended up going airborne signal which satisfied my infantry/signal ambivalence.

First Semester Roommate

My fall roommate was Mike Goff who hailed from Ashland, Kentucky. Mike was short in stature, barely meeting the minimum height requirement to be a cadet. That didn't stop Mike from successfully meeting all of West Point's physical challenges. The one area that gave him trouble was plebe-year survival swimming. Cadets that could not swim or were poor swimmers, were assigned to the "rock squad" where they were given remedial swimming lessons before having to pass the survival swim test, and Mike was on the "rock squad." One of the survival tests you had to pass was being able to tread water for 10 minutes with a brick in your backpack and supporting a 9.5 pound rifle over your head. For Mike, the weight of the brick and the rifle were much more relative to his body weight. When it was Mike's turn, no matter how hard he kicked and paddled with his free hand, it was a losing battle, and he would gradually sink. The pool was 8' deep and at the bottom of his trajectory, Mike would bound off the bottom, gasping for air as his head emerged from the water. The rest of the class was standing alongside the pool, helplessly observing. When some of us started to make a move towards the pool to help Mike, our instructor, Mr. Sorge, aggressively motioned for us to stand back, saying, "There are no walls out there!" Somehow Mike passed.

Mike was very smart and would join the Corps of Engineers upon graduation. One day while we had a few moments before lunch formation, I took out my guitar, and started strumming some chords as I looked out the window, facing north over the Plain. Outside the weather was cold, the sky was grey, and it was starting to drizzle. The chords and bad weather combined to inspire me to write a song. I jotted down the first verse so I wouldn't forget it.

> Hopped in my car, turned on the radio.
> Listened to the weather report, it went like so.
> Cold winds from the north, driving rain killing frost.
> A cold winds gonna blow over me.

Mike, ever the engineer, commented that it was impossible to have rain and killing frost at the same time. To which I answered, "Mike, It's poetic license." I was company first sergeant and had to go to formation to receive the report. The other verses would have to wait until later that night.

Fall and Winter Intramurals

As first classmen, we decided who in the company would be on which intramural team. In the fall, I chose to play 8-man tackle football for a second time. In the winter I wrestled for a second season. This time I was undefeated, having been taught in the offseason how to use my legs more effectively, so I didn't have to rely solely on my good upper-body strength.

Football: Army vs Penn State

In mid-October Army played Penn State again, this time at Beaver Stadium on their campus. The upper two classes made the trip. The Army team unveiled a different formation for this game, featuring large gaps between the linemen. We were going to run the ball, virtually every play, relying on cross blocks and traps to open large holes for the running backs to exploit. It worked. Our quarterback Rollie Stichweh (Class of 1965) and fellow member of Company B-2, played a great game and we won 10-7, beating Penn State for the third time in a row. We spent the time after the game on campus. The Penn State student body was very friendly to us. All fraternities were open to us with drinks on the house.

Football: Army vs Air Force

The first ever Army-Air Force game was played in Chicago, on November 2nd, 1963. We took the train from West Point to Chicago Union Station. The commandeered cars were so old we joked that they still had arrows stuck in the sides. The game was held at Soldiers' Field, where the NFL Bears played, and it was only a short march from Union Station. Army prevailed, winning 14-10. During the game, some Air Force cadets waved a large banner, reading "A M F," which we realized meant "Adios mother f____er." After the game, we had until midnight to explore Chicago on our own. As we were leaving the stadium, a newspaper reporter asked a nearby cadet what "A M F" meant. The quick-witted cadet responded, "Army mashes Falcons." At the end of the evening, walking back to Union Station, we passed a newspaper stand with the early edition on display. The headline read, "Army Mashes Falcons."

President Kennedy's Assassination

November 22, 1963. As we were walking back from class in Thayer Hall, we were approached by a number of cadets running towards us. They had been studying in their rooms and heard on the radio that President Kennedy had been shot. Later it was announced that he had died.

Everyone was in shock. On a personal level, we didn't know how this would affect us. At that moment the West Point administration was seeking direction from the Department of Defense. It was like everyone hit the pause button. Afternoon classes and intramurals were cancelled, as was football practice for the upcoming Army-Navy game, originally scheduled to be played November 30th.

The next day classes were resumed and a contingent of cadets was dispatched to participate in Kennedy's funeral. We didn't know if the Army-Navy game was cancelled or to be rescheduled.

John Kennedy had served in World War II as a Navy patrol boat captain. He was a Navy man, and especially fond of the Army – Navy game. It was the Kennedy family decision to reschedule the game one week, to December 7th which coincidently was the day Pearl Harbor had been attacked by the Japanese in WWII.

The Great Mess Hall Riot

The all-male cheerleaders were called the "Rabble Rousers." (The first women cadets did not enter West Point until 1976.) The "Rabble Rousers" rode the Army mules, fired the ceremonial 75mm howitzer after Army scored, and led us in cheers at the games and at rallies. Someone decided that our spirit was peaking too soon in the season, so in the fall of 1963, the rallies in Washington Hall (the mess hall) were less fueled than in previous years, until Army-Navy week. The week before the Army-Navy game the pent-up energy exploded at the mess hall rally.

Our dining tables were constructed of heavy oak and large enough to seat ten people. In spite of their size and weight, the tables were being stacked four high, one on top of the other. The table stacks were being carried and moved about by the tables' occupants, with one of the occupants on the top waving his tunic or napkin. The table stacks were moving about like opposing battle ships. Table accessories were being tossed from one area to another like hand grenades.

When it was over, we were told to return to our barracks. The cadet leadership and Rabble Rousers were summoned to Washington Hall to meet with the officer in charge that day, who happened to be our TAC officer, Major Rogers, who I suspect saw his career coming to an end that night, but there really was nothing he could have done. Some damage has been done to Washington Hall. Rather punish the entire Corps (or ruin Maj. Roger's career) it was decided to assess everyone a small amount that was taken from our cadet bank account.

The Three Amigos in Philadelphia

With so many upperclassmen taking leave that weekend and all headed to Philadelphia, Greyhound scheduled a bus to take us straight to Philadelphia. This was a good deal for us and a good deal for the bus company. Eddie Sims, George Cromartie and I took advantage of this charted bus to Philadelphia. It was not free. We had to pay for our tickets.

We checked into the same hotel, with George and I sharing a room. Eddie's fiancé Jean had to work Friday and would drive herself to the game on Saturday morning.

After checking in, the 'three amigos" headed out on foot, in civilian clothes, to explore Philadelphia. We passed a crowded bar and decided to check it out. The room was long and narrow with a bar running the entire length of the room. We had to push our way to the bar to get our drinks. At the back of the room there were stairs leading to another room upstairs. It was so crowded, we decided to try the upstairs room. We were only there a minute when Eddie said, "Let's go." I objected because we hadn't even finished our first drink. Eddie then said, "Look around." When I did, I noticed the bar clientele were all men. It was a gay bar. We retreated the way we had come in, pushing our way back down the stairs and the length of the downstairs room to the front door.

The 1963 Army – Navy Game

Navy quarterback, future All-American and NFL star, Roger Staubach would dominate the first half. But the second half was a different story with the Army defense keeping Roger in check and the Army offense clawing its way back into the game, twice driving the length of the field to score.

The Navy team seemed worn out and could not stop Army. Late in the game, the Army team drove the length of the field again, down to the 2-yard line. The whole stadium was going nuts. Stichweh indicated to the referee that he could not hear, and the referee signaled time out. Based on the referee's signal, the Army team decided to re-huddle. While they were in the huddle, the referee started the clock again and as Army broke the huddle, the cannon went off indicating that time had run out and the game was over. The final score was 15-21, with Army losing to Navy for the fourth year in a row.

A year later, we were 2nd lieutenants in the Army, when Rollie Stichweh had his revenge and led his Army team to defeat Staubach's favored Navy team 11-8.

Stranded in Philadelphia.

Jean and Eddie linked up after the game. George and I were dateless stags, getting progressively more sloshed as we visited hotel room parties in our hotel and other hotels where classmates were staying.

My role as company First Sergeant extended through the Army-Navy game, not a day longer.

When we got back to our hotel room, while George was in the bathroom, I cut the First Sergeant diamond off my overcoat, as I was no longer the company First Sergeant. When I awoke the next morning George was gone. He was a member of the Protestant Choir, and they were performing somewhere that night. Also gone was my long overcoat with my wallet, ID and money in its inner pocket. Without the First Sergeant diamond, George had mistakenly taken my overcoat to be his own.

An instant feeling of panic swept over me. In those days there were no cell phones and no credit cards, and here I was in Philadelphia with no money to pay my hotel room, nor to pay for a bus ride back to West Point. When I went to the hotel desk to explain, they were very understanding, and not concerned about me stiffing them for the two-day room bill. They knew my "home address" and they would bill me at West Point.

The next problem was getting transportation back to West Point. I hung around the lobby hoping to see a classmate who had not left yet and could provide me a ride back to West Point. Classmate and fellow B-2 cadet, John Duffy appeared, and his girlfriend drove us both back to West Point.

Christmas Leave, December 1963

When I got home on Christmas leave, I called Joan. Her mother answered the phone and advised me that "Joan was out for the evening," and asked me, "Should I leave a message?" I declined.

One night I went to the movies in Glen Cove with my cousin Danny Walsh, and afterwards we went to "Molly and Me's," a nearby college hangout. Unbeknownst to me, Joan was there with her friend Albert, who she knew from high school honors classes. When Joan spotted me at the bar, she came over and asked me why I didn't call again, to which I responded, "I can't handle it," which was the truth. She was very attractive and popular, and I could not handle waiting in line for a "maybe" relationship.

14

First Class Year, Second Semester

Second Semester Roommates

First Class year, the rank and positions in the company differed between first and second semesters. First semester I had been the company First Sergeant. Second semester George Cromartie would hold that position.

George and I roomed together second semester. Our first semester roommates, Mike Goff and Eddie Sims, were assigned to battalion staff. This was an easy transition for us as we were all good friends. George was a southern boy from Raleigh, North Carolina. He had a unique, dry sense of humor that was greatly appreciated by all of us. He saw the humor in just about everything and could, in real time, provide a comic script for the reality we were witnessing.

Weekend Leave

As yearlings we had been authorized one weekend leave per semester, and two weekends per semester as Cows. As Firsties, we were authorized 11 weekend leaves for the academic year, regardless of the semester. A weekend leave actually was only an 18-hour pass, as you couldn't leave West Point until after Saturday morning parade, and you had to be back for supper formation at 6:20 pm.

After Saturday morning parade, I took the Greyhound Bus to New York City and then the subway to Brooklyn, where there was a discount music store we heard about. My mission was to buy myself a Fender Stratocaster guitar and Fender bass for Kenny Waldrop, who had given me his money ahead of time. The music store was more like a warehouse with floor-to-ceiling racks filled with guitars. I don't know how we knew about this place.

Joan had instructed me to take the subway from Brooklyn to Queens where she worked, and she would drive us home from there. I took the subway, carrying the two instrument cases. When I tried to wedge the bass case into the back of her TR-3 it cracked her rear window. She reminds me that she never complained about this.

Army vs Johns Basketball Game

Army was scheduled to play the St. Johns basketball team on February 15th, and I invited Joan to come to West Point for the game. Her parents drove her from Long Island. They regularly attended St. John's home games, and I think they were curious about seeing West Point. My cousin Chris and her future husband Bruce McCormick attended St. Johns and were driving up to see the game as well.

I recall Joan's father was interested in following the career of Bobby McIntyre who had been Joan's freshman-year boyfriend and was now a starting forward as a sophomore.

The game was played in the fieldhouse, where a floor-to-ceiling net bisected the space, with the basketball court and bleachers occupying the west end. During the week, the fieldhouse was a buzz of activity, with the basketball team practicing at their end, the pre-season baseball and lacrosse teams splitting time at the other end, and the track team running laps around all of us.

Incidentally, Army won the game 67-64 over the favored Redmen.

Joan's parents drove home immediately after the game and Joan elected to drive home later with Chris and Bruce who were staying to hear our band, playing our regular Saturday night gig at the Weapons Room. While we were playing, Joan sat in a booth with Chris and Bruce, where she was approached by other cadets, requesting a dance. All Joan had to say was "I am dating a Firstie" and the underclassmen would slither away. If a classmate tried to hustle someone's date, they would be labeled as a "snake," and socially ostracized by their classmates, but that did not stop everyone. I made sure this night our sets were short, and our breaks were long. The juke box provided the music between our sets, and I was able to dance with Joan during our breaks.

When we emerged from the Weapons Room after our gig was over, we discovered it had been snowing. Rather than attempting to drive the considerable distance in a snowstorm, Chris and Bruce wisely decided to check into the Hotel Thayer to wait out the storm. Joan did likewise and the three of them departed West Point after attending Mass the next day.

The 100 Night Show

The annual "100 Night Show" celebrated that there were only 100 days until graduation. This year's rendition was produced and performed by OUR Class, to celebrate OUR graduation. As always, the play was a spoof of cadet life.

One of the characters portrayed (maybe in a previous show) was Major Parmly, who had been the TAC officer of Company G-2. "Ranger Parmly," as he was known, was a "gung-ho" infantryman who took G-2 on pre-reveille runs until the academic departments intervened and put an end to that. The character in the play had a foot-long "Ranger Tab" on his uniform.

The Car Show

Every year a car show was conducted in the fieldhouse, with local dealerships exhibiting their models for the year. Only the dealerships offering the best discounts were invited to the exhibition. This event was advantageous for both the dealers and for the first classmen, who were in the market for buying a new car before graduation and could view all the new cars in one place. I fell in love with the marimba red Pontiac Le Mans convertible on display and that's what I ordered.

Spring Lacrosse

Before spring lacrosse practice, Coach Jim Adams invited four Firsties, me being one of them, to meet with him in his office at different times. We were each told that we would not be on that year's varsity team, having been supplanted by four very talented Cows, who had been recruited to play lacrosse, moving up from B Squad (JV). Coach Adams was a true gentleman. He took the time to break the news to us in person, one at a time, rather than just posting the roster without our names on it. He thanked us for having been part of the program. I still remember the names of my three classmates that were cut with me, and the four Cows that replaced us

The next day, I was nominated by my B-2 classmates to be B-2's intramural lacrosse player/coach. I packed the team with my classmates and friends: Jack Richards, Larry Strickland, Bob Monson, Dwight Raymond, Eddie Sims, and George Cromartie among others.

General MacArthur's Funeral

General MacArthur died April 5, 1964, and the entire Corps was bused to NYC to march in his funeral parade. He would have liked that.

We've Got Wheels!

In mid-April our shiny new cars were delivered and parked on Buffalo Solders' Field, across the street from the Hotel Thayer. As Firsties we were authorized 11 weekend leaves for the academic year, and we horded those 30-hour passes until after we received our cars. The only stipulation was that you had to be passing all your subjects and a skeleton crew of Firsties had to be present for the Saturday Parade and to maintain some degree of law and order within the company. Once the cars arrived, half the First Class would be gone on any given weekend. The company XO might be filling in for the CO, the first sergeant might be filling in for the XO, and the platoon sergeants filling in for the platoon leaders.

The 1964 World's Fair

One of the most popular destinations was the 1964 World's Fair, situated on Long Island, northeast of the intersection of Grand Central Parkway and the L.I.E (Long Island Expressway). Riding with me in my car were George Cromartie, Larry Strickland and wife-to-be Sally

Chapman. I was selected to drive since I was from Long Island and the others believed I would know how to get there. It was a beautiful, sunny, hot day so we ventured forth with the top down. I was confident in my navigation skills: Palisades Parkway to the Tappan Zee Bridge, to the Cross Bronx Expressway, to the Whitestone Bridge to Grand Central Parkway. I knew the route. How hard could it be to find the World's Fair?

As we progressed along Grand Central Parkway, we could see the World's Fair Globe to our left, but there was no way to get there directly off the Grand Central. I correctly concluded that access to the World's Fair had to come from the L.I.E.

The intersection with the L.I.E. was a maze of cloverleaf exit ramps. I took the exit ramp for the "L.I.E. EAST." What I didn't realize was that only the left lane put you onto the L.I.E. If you were in the right lane, which we were, you were looped around and put back on the Grand Central, heading back towards the Whitestone Bridge. I didn't have time to change lanes, and fortunately, by simply staying in the right lane, we looped through all four cloverleafs, and ended up back on Grand Central, approaching the L.I.E. underpass once again. There was no time to analyze what had just happened to us. I immediately put on my right turn signal and took the "L.I.E. EAST" exit ramp once again, hoping to discover where we went wrong the first time. By this point we were all laughing hysterically at our predicament, and someone started us singing the Kingston Trio song about poor Charlie getting lost on the M.T.A. "He was lost forever 'neath the streets of Boston. He was the man who never returned."

Staying the in the right lane put us on the L.I.E. heading east as intended. Once on the L.I.E. we could see the entrance to the World's

Fair was off the westbound lane of the L.I.E. and a turnaround had been constructed to get there from the eastbound lane.

Armed Forces Weekend

On Saturday the Corps marched in New York City's Armed Forces Day parade. (I didn't march the previous year as we had been playing Hofstra in lacrosse that day.) This year, I took Joan to Trader Vic's for dinner Saturday night, and after dinner we went to see Ray Charles at Carnegie Hall. After the concert we attended a hotel room party, with music provided by a portable record player. I remember Joan was wearing a red dress and the song was "Could This Be Magic."

Open House at 33 Emerson Rd.

In the spring, half the Firsties would be on weekend leave, driving their new cars someplace away from the confines of West Point. New York City was a popular destination, but that was expensive, and usually limited to a one-time event. Only a few guys had girl friends that lived within driving distance. The others were eager for a place to go.

The weekend before June Week, I brought home my guitar, amplifier, and stereo. During the week I spread the word amongst my B-2 classmates that there would be "open house" at my parents' house Saturday night. We had a good turnout and our driveway looked like a car dealership. When I awoke from sleeping in my own bed, I discovered a couple of guys sleeping on the living room floor and some others sleeping in their cars. By mid-afternoon Sunday, all the cars were gone.

June Week, 1964

June Week officially began on Saturday, May 30th and ended with our graduation on June 3rd.

The intercollegiate spring sports were lacrosse, baseball, track tennis and golf, and all had their Army-Navy game on the Saturday of June week, with the site of the games alternating annually between the two academies. This year baseball would be at Annapolis and lacrosse would be at West Point. We won baseball and the majority of games but lost to the Midshipmen in lacrosse. We had beaten them the year before, but this was to be Navy's year and they were crowned national champions.

I invited Joan to come to West Point for June Week, but she could not come up for the whole 5-day affair as she was a bridesmaid in Ginny Murphy's wedding that weekend.

The day after the wedding, I drove my new Pontiac Le Mans to Long Island to pick her up. This was a risky move as the "Alumni Review" (parade) was scheduled for that afternoon and it was imperative that I be there in time for pre-parade formation. I would have been in deep trouble If my car broke down or I had gotten into an accident and missed the parade. I got back to West Point without incident. While we were getting ready for the parade, Joan linked up with Jean, Sally and Marie, the crew of girls dating Eddie Sims, Larry Strickland, and Dwight Raymond.

The Alumni Review

Each year, there are two "Alumni Reviews." One to honor the classes celebrating their reunions June Week, and the other to honor the classes celebrating their reunions homecoming weekend in the fall.

The "Alumni Review" was a big deal for the alumni and for us. This was our last as cadets.

In the American Civil War, 2/3 of the battles were commanded on both sides by West Pointers. The Association of Graduates was established in 1869 to invite graduates, who had fought for the Confederacy, back to West Point for a reunion with their classmates. The music for the Alumni Review was, and is, a composite of northern and southern songs dating back to that conflict. The march opens with "When Johnny Comes Marching Home Again."

The alumni assembled on the roadway between the barracks and the southern edge of the Plain. The opening strains "When Johnny Comes Marching Home Again" signaled them to start marching onto the Plain, with the oldest class leading the way. The alumni took their positions, lining the west side of the parade field of the Plain. When it came time to "pass in review," we saluted them with a long "eyes right," all the while them eyeing us and we were eyeing them, the "long grey line."

Social Events

Besides June Week athletic events and parades, there were two main social events, An afternoon "Tea" in the Superintendent's Garden, and the First Class Ball.

The First Class Ball was held in Washington Hall, the evening before the Graduation Parade. The Ball was a very formal, long gown affair for the ladies and entailed navigating a long receiving line of dignitaries. The protocol was to introduce yourself and your date to the first person in line, usually a general's aide, and that person would introduce you to the first dignitary. As you proceeded down the line, the spouse of each dignitary would introduce you to the next dignitary in line. Being a general's wife required having good hearing and a good memory.

The graduating Firsties were expected to make a "call" on the Superintendent, General Lampert, and his wife. (General Lampert had replaced General Westmoreland at the beginning of our Firstie year.)

The Superintendent's house faced the Plain. It was on a cozy, corner plot, with the gym on the opposite side of Brewerton Road, and north area barracks on the opposite side of Scott Place. The house faced the Plain. A 6 ft. stone wall provided privacy from the gym and the cadet barracks.

The companies were scheduled for overlapping times, and we were expected to stay about 10 minutes, to make room for the next company. There was a receiving line and our TAC officer, Major Rogers, was there to introduce us to the Superintendent and his wife. We were expected to leave our "calling cards" on a platter, obviously positioned for that purpose. This was an Army tradition that would be repeated when we arrived at our regular Army battalions. Iced tea and fruit punch were served and were welcomed as it was a hot day. Mrs. Lampert offered to take us on a tour of the house and showed us the basement room where a ghost allegedly materialized. That room was preserved as it was in the 1800s, with a desk and bed reserved for the ghost. When we asked her if she had seen the ghost she just shrugged.

Graduation Parade

As always, the Graduation Parade was held late afternoon, the day before graduation. Once the Corps had assembled on the Plain, and reports rendered, the First Classmen were directed to march, individually, forward to the westside of the parade field. This was the moment, our class surrendered command of the Corps to the Cows, the class behind us, the Class of 1965.

We took up our position on the right side of the parade field to receive the "Eyes Right!" salute as the Corps passed in review. We all looked for our own companies, making eye contact with the Cows who were now leading the Companies, B-2 in my case.

The West Point Army Band played the Graduation March which begins with "There's No Place Like Home" being played slowly. The march tempo picks up with samples of "100 Night's 'til June", "The Corps", "Mendelssohn's Wedding March", "Hell Cat Reveille" and "Auld Lang Syne."

The medley hit me like a ton of bricks. I had been so looking forward to graduation, I hadn't given much thought about the reality that our time at West Point was coming to an end, and our class being dispersed. I wondered if I would see them again. Eddie and Jean were to be married the next day and as the saying goes, "wedding bells are breaking up that old gang of mine." I needed not worry as many of us would serve together at various Army posts, in Vietnam, visiting each other, and seeing each other at reunions. These would be my lifetime best friends.

After the parade came the "Recognition" of the Plebes in our Company, the Class of 1967. The Class of 1965 was now in charge of the Corps, and we had no other responsibilities, other than to show up for graduation the next morning. That night, a half-dozen of us and our dates had dinner at a nice, candlelight restaurant on Highway 9W, south of Highland Falls. (The restaurant is no longer there.)

The Graduation Ceremony

We graduated June 3, 1964. The ceremony was held, mid-morning, in the Field House. We were dressed in full dress grey uniforms, complete with sabers and red sashes. We were seated in class-order-of-merit and called to the stage in that order.

One of the unwritten traditions at West Point was that every member of the graduating class contributed $1 to the man who would graduate last in the class. This honored position was referred to as the "Goat." Our beloved "Goat" was Tucker Dooley, who had occupied the "ejection seat" for four years, with guys ranked above him being "found" (eliminated) each semester.

The guest speaker was Stephen Ailes, Secretary of the Army, which was a little disappointing, in that President Kennedy had delivered the 1962 address and General Maxwell Taylor, then Chairman of the Joint Chiefs of Staff, had delivered the 1963 address.

We were each provided six guest tickets and mine went to my mom and dad, sister, brother-in-law, Joan and my grandpa, William Nesbitt Robertson Sr. The ticket for my grandpa was a nice gesture on my part, as he was in failing health and I didn't expect he would be able to come. I underestimated his determination. He had to quit high school to support his sisters when they were orphaned and seeing William III graduate from West Point was a big deal for him. My grandpa died a few months later.

Eddie and Jean's Wedding

After the graduation ceremony, Joan accompanied me back to the barracks, where I would change from my Full Dress Grey cadet uniform into my brand new Army Blues for Eddie and Jean Sims' wedding, scheduled for that afternoon. We parked my new car inside Central Area, which would never be tolerated any other day. I invited Joan to come into the barracks with me rather than her having to wait in the car by herself. When we got to my floor, Rich Leary, class of 1965, nonchalantly stroll past us on his way to the shower at the end of the hall, with only a towel wrapped around his waist, like seeing a girl in the barracks was a normal thing.

I had been given second lieutenant gold bars by my Uncle Bob Lambert and by Chuck Hines who was a first lieutenant I served with in Germany the previous summer. Bob had been a lieutenant in the NY National Guard. Both had told me they would be honored if I would wear their gold bars. I did not have a "pinning ceremony" graduation day, as they might have envisioned, but I did proudly wear their gold bars when I reported to Fort Benning for Airborne School.

The afternoon of our graduation, I was one of four ushers for Eddie and Jean Sim's wedding at the Cadet Chapel, which was up the hill, overlooking the barracks and the Plain. The other ushers were George Cromartie, Bernie Ferry, and Larry Bedell. After the ceremony, the four of us raised sabers as Eddie and Jean emerged from the Chapel and they proceeded down the front steps under our arched sabers. The Wedding Reception was at the Officers' Club, overlooking the Hudson River.

Finishing Touches

Rather than proceeding straight home to Raleigh, North Carolina, George Cromartie stayed overnight at my parents' house on Long Island. The next day, the two of us drove to Ohio where we would be ushers in the weddings of Chris and Nancy Bast, and Tom and Mary Jane Cunningham. Joan and I would be married July 12, 1969, after my back-to-back tours in Southeast Asia.

CPSIA information can be obtained
at www.ICGtesting.com
Printed in the USA
LVHW082029231122
733501LV00018BA/1281